THE 1960s

Sally Hewitt

W
FRANKLIN WATTS
LONDON•SYDNEY

I can remember the 1960s

First published in 2003 by Franklin Watts
96 Leonard Street, London EC2A 4XD

Franklin Watts Australia
45-51 Huntley Street
Alexandria, NSW 2015

© Franklin Watts 2003

Series editor: Sarah Peutrill
Series design: White Design
Art director: Jonathan Hair
Picture researcher: Diana Morris

A CIP catalogue record
for this book is available from
the British Library

ISBN 0 7496 4867 8

Printed in Malaysia

Picture credits:
Advertising Archives: 9b. Bettmann/Corbis: 25. Central
Press/Hulton Archive: 17t. Chatter/RHPL: 19t.
Cranham/Fox/Hulton: 28. Mary Evans PL: 11b. Evening
Standard/Hulton Archive: 12b. Fox/Hulton Archive: 13b. Caroline
Gilles/BIPS/Hulton Archive: 21. Tim Graham/Fox/Hulton Archive: 20. Hulton Archive:
front cover cr, 15b, 16, 23. Keystone/Hulton Archive: 8b, 9t, 27. Lensart/Mary Evans PL:
11b. Albert McCabe/Express/Hulton Archive: 29. Edward Miller/Keystone/Hulton Archive:
15t. NASA: 24. Popperfoto: front cover tl. Roy/Hulton Archive: 7b. Ted Streshinksy/Corbis:
front cover b. Waterman/Fox/Hulton Archive: 4t.

The author and publisher would like to thank everyone who contributed
their memories and personal photographs to this book.

Contents

Introduction

The 1960s
During the years after the end of World War II in 1945, there was a rise in the birth rate in Britain and America which became known as 'the baby boom'. By the 1960s 'baby boomers' were young people with money to spend. They set new trends in music and fashion and challenged the authority of the older generation.

⬆ The Berlin Wall was built in 1961 to prevent people living in communist East Berlin from moving to the more prosperous West Berlin.

Music

Young people already had their own music – Elvis Presley and rock 'n' roll. In 1962 a Liverpool band called the Beatles released the single 'Love Me Do' and started a new phenomenon – Beatlemania. Screaming teenage fans greeted them wherever they went and for the rest of the decade they influenced not only music but fashion and even the political ideas of young people all over the world.

Fashion

New fashions broke all the old rules. The fashion designer Mary Quant introduced miniskirts, tights and straight hair for girls. Boys grew their hair and swapped their shirts and ties for polo-neck sweaters.

Unforgettable events

The 1960s was a decade of unforgettable events that shocked or amazed the world. In 1961 the Berlin Wall was built and became a symbol of the so-called 'iron curtain' that divided communist Eastern Europe from the democratic West. In 1963, America's president John F Kennedy was assassinated. In 1969 the American Neil Armstrong became the first person to walk on the moon. Anyone who was alive at the time will probably remember, even today, where they were when these events happened.

Revolution

Different groups tried to change the world through peaceful protest. Martin Luther King campaigned for equal rights for black Americans. French students challenged their government and brought Paris to a standstill. In America students protested against their country's involvement in the Vietnam War.

They can remember

In this book six people share their memories of what it was like to live in Britain in the 1960s. They each have a story to tell in their own section, but they also add other memories throughout the book.

Then

Now

Sue Anderson
Sue, the daughter of Jamaican immigrants, grew up in south London in the 1960s.

Valerie Beeby
Valerie lived and worked in 'Swinging London' and remembers the changes in fashions.

Then

Now

Then

Alasdair Meldrum
Alasdair grew up in Dumfries in Scotland in the 1960s.

Then

Now

Mike and Tony Cook
Mike and Tony were teenagers during the 1960s. They went to the 1966 World Cup.

Now

John Bowden
John remembers going to a Beatles' concert when he was a teenager growing up in Prestbury in Cheshire.

Then

Now

Diana Caryl*
Diana grew up in a coal-mining town in south Wales.

* Now Diana Rowland

Then

Now

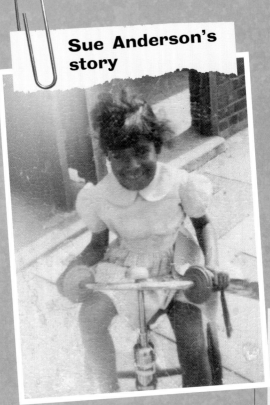

Sue Anderson's story

Sue, 1963

Childhood games
· · · · · · · · · · · · · · · · · · · ·

Here are some of the games Sue used to play in the 1960s:

➡ Knock down ginger (knocking on doors and running away)

➡ French skipping (a game where you jump over elastic that is tied around two standing people)

➡ Leapfrog down the road

➡ Bouncing two balls against the wall to rhymes

➡ Hopscotch on the pavement

CHILDHOOD IN WANDSWORTH
Sue's parents arrived in Britain from Jamaica in the early 1950s with Sue's two older brothers and sister. They settled down in Wandsworth in south London. Sue was born in London in 1958 and her sister Hyacinth was born one year later.

THINGS LEFT BEHIND
When Sue's parents left Jamaica, they left their home, their work, their family and even their name behind.

> *When my parents were coming over on the ship the captain said, 'Take my name,' (which was Anderson). 'They are not going to be able to pronounce your name in London.'*

PUBLIC BATHS
Sue's house, like many others in Wandsworth, didn't have a bathroom when they moved in. The public baths was not where you went for a swim; you went there for a hot bath.

> *The public baths used to be very steamy. People would go down there with their towels to have a bath, especially at the weekends.*

NEW BATHROOM
Sue's father wanted the family to have their own bathroom.

> *A lot of houses just had a tin bath in the scullery. My dad had a shower in Jamaica so he built a bathroom for us here in our scullery.*

CREEPY CRAWLIES

Outside toilets – at the bottom of the garden – were common in the 1960s.

> 66 My sister and I were frightened of going outside in the dark and seeing creepy crawlies in the toilet. My parents said, 'It's much worse in Jamaica. The creepy crawlies are bigger and there are snakes!' 99

PLAYING OUTSIDE

Sue always felt safe playing outside on the pavement with other children in the neighbourhood.

> 66 When the children wanted a change from playing in the street, they could go to the local park on Garratt Lane.
>
> You could borrow pogo sticks, hula hoops, stilts, skipping ropes, footballs and cricket bats. It was free. You just had to put them all back in the hut when you had finished. We played in the park for hours. 99

➡ Pogo sticks required practice and good balance. The idea was to bounce up and down and stay on!

NEW OPPORTUNITIES

Sue's parents wanted the girls to have opportunities they didn't have themselves. They sent them to Brownies where they learnt to swim, and to Sunday school.

> 66 We went to a Catholic Sunday school, but we weren't even Catholic. It was a church so my parents just sent us there. We didn't understand what they were talking about. Mum would say, 'What did you learn?' We said, 'We don't know!' 99

Family life

NUCLEAR FAMILY

In the 1960s, the ideal family was a married couple living together with their children. Unlike previous generations, they probably did not live nearby grandparents, aunts and uncles as the father may have moved away from home to find work. This small family unit was called the 'nuclear family'.

HOUSEWORK AND COOKING

It was usual for the mother to stay at home and look after the family while the father went out to work. Although washing machines and other household appliances were becoming more affordable, housework and cooking still took up much more time than they do today.

FAMILY MEALS

Alasdair, his brother and sister and his dad all came home from school and the office for lunch, which was the main meal of the day.

> " *My mum would cook at least a two-course meal for lunch, from scratch, using basic ingredients. The only people who had school lunches were the children who came in from outlying farms and just couldn't get home.* "

In 1961 a woman spent over 12 hours a week cleaning and doing the laundry, and about 1 hour 40 minutes a day cooking. Diana remembers coming home from school.

> " *Mum would be in the kitchen, baking or cooking dinner, or working in the garden. We'd have dinner as soon as Dad got home from work, about six o'clock.* "

← Many families in the 1960s had tea in the early evening, usually with bread and jam.

PARENTAL CONTROL

Alasdair remembers that his parents wanted to have much more control over his life than he expected to have over his own children. When he grew his hair and played in a rock band, it was a way of rebelling against his parents without upsetting them too much.

> " *I was very fond of my family and I wasn't going to do anything that would truly distance myself from them. I was just making my point.* "

The long-haired Beatles' look was popular with young people.

TELEVISION

Television was becoming part of family life, but unlike today, it was not automatic for everyone to have one. Among his friends Alasdair was one of the last to get a television.

> " Dr Who *was a cult even then. Everyone was watching it and everyone was talking about it. We felt really out of it because we didn't have a television. My parents thought that if we got one it would ruin family life. They held out against buying one for some time.* "

Diana remembers...
"*I wasn't allowed to watch any television until homework was finished satisfactorily.*"

The 1968 Olympics encouraged some people to buy a colour television for the first time.

Colour television

For most of the 1960s, television was still in black and white and there were only two channels. In 1967, the first colour television broadcasts in Britain were transmitted. By September 1968, 100,000 homes had colour televisions.

John remembers...
"*We got a colour TV in 1969. Dad was a snooker fan. Now he could see all the coloured balls.*"

The excitement, drama and colour of the Olympics brought to life by the HMV Colourmaster

HMV put quality first

25"
£362.18s.

Growing up in Scotland

LIVING IN DUMFRIES

Alasdair was brought up in Dumfries in south-west Scotland. His father organised physical education in their local area. His mother stayed at home and looked after Alasdair and his older brother and younger sister. Dumfries is on the River Nith, surrounded by hills and farms.

> *It was a very beautiful place to be brought up. Many of my friends lived on farms. They came quite a long way into school or even stayed in a hostel from Monday to Friday.*

PROUD TO BE SCOTTISH

Alasdair was brought up to be proud of being Scottish. The first time he travelled outside Scotland was on a Scout trip to Norway. He had to apply for a passport.

> *I was asked to put down what nationality I was. I put down Scottish. But there is no such thing. Correctly, I should have put British, but in those days, that was how I felt and how all my friends felt.*

Alasdair Meldrum's story

Alasdair, 1960

⬇ Dumfries in the 1960s.

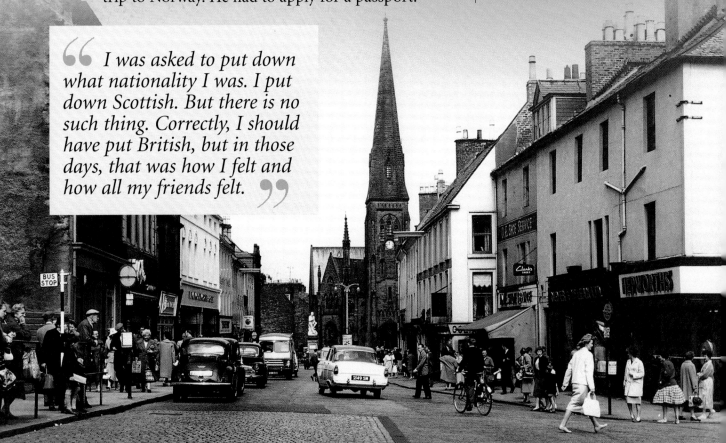

PREJUDICE

It was difficult for English pupils to fit in.

> We did have the odd person in our school who was English. They had to be twice as good as the average simply to fit in. There was quite a lot of prejudice against the English based on hundreds of years of feeling that they had tried to dominate us.

Alasdair at university, 1967

CHOICE OF UNIVERSITY

Alasdair shocked his careers' teacher when he told him his choice of university, even though it was in Scotland.

> He said, 'Well, Alasdair, which of the two great universities do you plan to apply for, Edinburgh or Glasgow?' I said, 'No, I'm going to go to St Andrew's. It's the best in the UK for applied maths.' He said, 'What! St Andrew's! You don't want to go there, it's full of English!'

But Alasdair has always felt his decision broadened his outlook on life.

KILTS

As a child Alasdair wore a traditional kilt on special occasions.

> The Scottish Highlanders used the kilt to put the fear of God into their enemies. I had a kilt when I was a little boy because everyone did. The tartan depends on what family you come from. Our family wears the Buchanan tartan.

BUCHANAN.

→ There are hundreds of types of tartan, distinguished by their different colours and stripe patterns. This is the Buchanan tartan.

> The only history I'd ever have learned was Scottish history. It was really important to have, by chance, gone to a university that opened my eyes to how much more there was to the world than just the bit north of Hadrian's Wall.

Education

SECONDARY SCHOOLS

In general, children of secondary-school age went to one of three types of school. If they passed the Eleven Plus exam they could go to a grammar school and were expected to go on to further education. Children who did not pass the Eleven Plus went to a secondary modern school or to one of a few technical schools which focused more on technical subjects and preparation for the world of work. During the 1960s and 1970s, this system was gradually phased out. In its place came comprehensive education, designed to cater for all children regardless of their ability.

⬆ Pupils at William Ellis School in London, 1962.

When John left Stockport Grammar School for Boys in 1962, his future had already been decided for him.

> *I had to go into the family business. My destination was decided regardless of my wishes, unless I was extremely strong-willed and went against it. I did my O' levels and that was it. If I wanted to further my education, I had to do it through day-release and night-school classes.*

SCHOOL UNIFORM

Diana remembers that school uniform could be embarrassing.

> *In winter we had to wear a blue felt hat, changing to a straw boater in summer. We had to wear a hat at all times when we were in school uniform, even on Saturdays after sports matches. I dreaded walking through Cardiff city centre, past Cardiff Arms Park on rugby match days, carrying a lacrosse stick!*

❗ Alasdair remembers ...
"School uniform was compulsory right through school and you would be sent home if you didn't turn up in the correct uniform."

RIVALRY

Alasdair passed his Eleven Plus and went to Dumfries Academy. He remembers there was friendly rivalry with the High School nearby.

> *When the snow fell there would be snowball fights between the Academy pupils in their maroon blazers and the High School pupils in their green blazers. We would pelt each other with snowballs. It was all good-natured but it was part of belonging to different schools.*

University

During the 1960s, only one person in twelve went to university and most of them were boys. But girls were gradually encouraged to attend university and new universities were built to accommodate more students. Today, one person in three goes to university and the girls outnumber the boys.

⬇ Construction work at the new University of Essex in 1966.

Diana left home and went to Southampton University in 1967.

"At first I found the work hard as I'd always been used to being near the top and here I was with loads of people who seemed so much cleverer and more assured. In the end, of course, they were fantastic times. I found it very quiet at home in the holidays and used to go back to university early 'to study'."

John Bowden's story

John, 1965

AN EXCITING DECADE

Children who had been in primary school during the 1950s, when family life and traditions were still much as they always had been, found that life as a teenager in the 1960s was very different. It was an exciting decade for teenagers. They had money to spend, grew their hair, wore shocking clothes and challenged adult authority. John and his friends wanted to be part of a new way of doing things.

MUSIC

In the 1960s, pop music expressed ideas that many adults found threatening.

> *Pop stars were singing songs with messages critical of people in power. There was a reaction from parents because they were challenging authority.*

The girls in John's group of friends liked American folk-rock singers Joan Baez and Bob Dylan, who wrote songs with a message. Their music didn't appeal to John.

> *I had a girlfriend and she and her friends used to analyse the songs and look for their inner meaning. I'd rather go and play Risk – a game where armies invade continents and you try to take over the world.*

! Alasdair remembers...

"I played the keyboards in a band called Sixth Order. My parents hated the whole thing because they thought I was mixing with a very bad lot. We did have a following of girls whom my mum wouldn't have wanted me to go out with."

THE BEATLES

The Beatles were four Liverpool lads – John, Paul, George and Ringo. They became the most successful band of all time. Hearing the Beatles on the radio for the first time is something John has never forgotten.

> *I remember I was in my room building with my Meccano set with a friend when we first heard the Beatles on the radio singing 'Please, Please Me'. Immediately, we knew it sounded completely different.*

↑ Excited Beatles' fans queue for tickets in Lewisham, south London, 1963.

John related to the Beatles' sound. He was from near Liverpool as well. He became a fan. In 1964, he went to a Beatles concert at the Apollo, Manchester. He remembers you couldn't buy tickets in advance.

↓ The 'Fab Four' – Ringo Starr, George Harrison, John Lennon and Paul McCartney.

> *We stood there in a long line of people and waited until the box office opened. There were lots of screaming girls. The Beatles seemed to encourage it. The girls in our group were screaming but the boys weren't. We thought, 'What's going on here?' People were jumping up and down, running around – it was strange behaviour we had never seen before.*

Wherever the Beatles went they were greeted by screaming fans. This became known as Beatlemania.

EVENTS IN AMERICA

Young people in Britain were not just concerned about events taking place on their doorstep. They looked over the Atlantic Ocean towards America. There, young Americans were being sent to fight a war far away from home in Vietnam, Dr Martin Luther King was campaigning for equal rights for black Americans, and hippies were asking the world to make love, not war.

I HAVE A DREAM

Black Americans still did not have the same civil rights as their fellow white Americans. In some areas they were not allowed to sit next to white people on buses or go to the same schools. In August 1963, Dr Martin Luther King gave a speech to 200,000 civil rights' marchers in Washington. He said,

> " *I have a dream that the sons of former slaves and the sons of former slave owners will be able to sit down together at the table of brotherhood.* "

Martin Luther King was awarded the Nobel Peace Prize in 1964. He was assassinated on 4th April 1968 in Memphis, Tennessee by James Earl Ray, an escaped convict.

WAR IN VIETNAM

America was fighting with South Vietnam against communist North Vietnam. Throughout the 1960s, the US became more and more involved and there were heavy casualties on all sides. Young people held anti-war demonstrations in America and in Britain. Despite this America did not withdraw from the war until 1973. South Vietnam struggled on alone until 1975 when it eventually surrendered.

⬇ Dr Martin Luther King delivers his 'I have a dream' speech in Washington.

HIPPIES

Hippies believed in 'flower power' and wanted to create a world based on peace and love. Sue, aged ten, was sitting with her mum and dad watching a hippie demonstration on the TV.

> " *I heard the hippies say, 'The world is coming to an end,' and I burst out crying. My parents said, 'What's the matter?' And I said, 'I don't want to go to Saturday Morning Pictures tomorrow.' They said, 'Why not?' I gave back the half a crown [12.5 pence] to my dad and said, 'If the world is going to end, then I want to be here with my mum and dad!'* "

→ John Lennon, one of the Beatles, and his wife Yoko Ono stayed in bed for a week to demonstrate for peace.

New opportunities

Young people were given more freedom than ever before, and this included the opportunity to travel and try new things. Valerie went travelling in America, but there were no mobile phones or internet cafés and getting in touch with home was a problem.

"I sent my parents a postcard to say that I was off to Acapulco instead of Mexico City. When I got back to New York two months later, I rang my mother, she said, 'Oh Valerie, I thought you were dead!' I sent the postcard in September. It arrived in February."

ⓘ John remembers...

"I did a parachute jump from 2,500 feet [760 metres]. You had to pack your own parachute. If you packed it wrong, it wouldn't open and it would be your responsibility. I only did it once."

17

Working woman

Valerie, 1962

ALL CHANGE

The 1950s had been a decade during which most people dressed formally and lived by established rules. During the 1960s there were sweeping changes in fashion, music and ideas that affected the whole of society. For Valerie, a young woman working in London, it was an exciting time.

> *The 1960s for me was dropping all the inhibitions and prim manners of the 1950s.*

LOWER PAY

In 1964, Valerie applied for a job at a big airline company. Her initial delight at getting the job was quickly dampened.

> *They told me afterwards that one of the reasons they gave me the job was that I was cheaper because they paid women less.*

⬇ In 1968, Valerie's work took her to America on an historic assignment. She was one of the first people to see the new Boeing jumbo jets. Valerie is standing near to the centre of the picture.

INEQUALITY

Valerie loved her job. She worked hard and started to travel, describing the places she visited for travel brochures. But despite doing well, she found it was difficult for women to be taken seriously. On one occasion, Valerie and her advertising manager's secretary were the only two women at a meeting. They were also the only two people in the room with a university degree.

> " *The advertising manager said, 'Of course we haven't got university calibre people in this department, we must do better.' It was as if we didn't exist, we weren't there.* "

↑ The King's Road in London in the 1960s.

SWINGING LONDON

London's King's Road and Carnaby Street were famous in the 1960s for their fashion boutiques. Valerie bought a flat on the King's Road and found herself living in the heart of 'Swinging London'. She suddenly became very popular.

> " *The King's Road was world-famous by then. Everybody was after me because I was living on the King's Road and everybody thought I was part of the 1960s. But one boyfriend dropped me when the 1960s' gloss wore off.* "

Fashion and style

SHOCKING FASHIONS

The older generation found the 1960s' fashions shocking. It was so different from what they were used to. Girls wearing miniskirts and boys with long hair made parents and teachers feel as if they were losing control. Young people enjoyed the sense of power they felt that their clothes, hairstyles and make-up were giving them.

MINISKIRTS

Mary Quant designed clothes that gave young women freedom of movement. Women threw away their uncomfortable suspender belts and tight skirts and swapped them for her miniskirts and matching tights.

! Diana remembers...

"I remember agonising over, and eventually buying, a very 1960s' Mary Quant sundress with bright colours, bold pattern and swirly skirt."

➡ The 1960s look: a miniskirt, boots and glamorous piled-high hair.

Valerie enjoyed the new fashions.

> " I bought the latest fashions and I used to parade up and down the corridors at work and watch the reactions. My skirts gradually crept higher and higher.
>
> I used to walk along the King's Road nearly every day and follow all the fashions. I might not go for three days and then I'd find another boutique had opened up. "

Even air stewardesses started to wear miniskirts.

> " I wrote the leaflets for air stewardesses advising them how to bend over discreetly in their miniskirts in the aircraft aisle. "

HAIR

Diana bought a fashionable nylon hair piece so that she could get the 1960s' look.

" *I have always had short hair and I wanted to pile it up on top and look glamorous! I don't remember wearing it more than a few times as it didn't feel like me and I didn't like feeling false. I'll never forget the joy and expectation with which I bought it, though.* "

FASHION FOR MEN

There were new fashions for men but it was hard for them to get rid of suits, ties and short hairstyles – especially if they were at work. Alasdair remembers how his clothes and hair upset his father.

" *One of the fashions was to wear a white vest showing underneath an open-necked shirt. My dad thought it was terrible because the only people he'd seen dressed like that were in Glasgow working in the dockyards. He couldn't understand why we wanted to look like that.* "

! John remembers...

"Not wearing a tie! Even now, I find it difficult to take my tie off. I'm often still wearing it at 11 at night. Instead of formal suits it was a black polo neck, a sports jacket, cord trousers and Hush Puppies."

Uniforms and Union Jacks

Valerie remembers that it wasn't only fashion that was shocking.

"There were all kinds of things that were thought to be outrageous like using the Union Jack on coffee mugs. People wore military uniforms who weren't entitled to them – that was thought to be shocking too."

→ Using the Union Jack as a design was thought to be disrespectful by some people.

21

Mike and Tony's story

Mike and Tony, 1966

⬇ Mike and Tony kept their souvenir brochure and the tickets for all the matches they attended.

CRAZY ABOUT FOOTBALL

Brothers Mike and Tony Cook were crazy about football. In 1966 when the World Cup football tournament came to England, Mike was 16 and Tony was 13.

Mike was determined to get to as many matches as he could – even if it meant missing school. Just before the World Cup began he was sent on a school field trip.

> *We were meant to be walking along the South Downs and collecting stuff on the local flora and fauna. Instead, we got into ticket queues at Wembley very early. I got to one or two of the early World Cup matches that way.*

ENGLAND'S PROGRESS

To the delight of every English football fan, the home team was doing well. They came top of their group, beat Argentina in the quarter-final and went on to beat Portugal in the semi-final. The final was between England and West Germany on 30th July.

THE FINAL

By that time term had ended, but Mike and Tony faced their biggest challenge so far – how could they get tickets for the final?

> *Our Uncle Colin, God bless his soul, knew how obsessed with football we were and set out to try and get us all tickets for the final. He could only get two. He just said, 'Look, you guys are total football fanatics, you have them.' I love him to this day.*

On the big day, they set out early. Tony remembers that they got to Wembley in good time to get a position at the front of the standing section.

> *The doors opened about 11 o' clock and we were there by 10, hanging about on the steps of Wembley. When the doors opened we went straight in, found our section and went right to the front. We had four hours to wait.*

MATCH REPORT

West Germany scored after 12 minutes. Six minutes later, Geoff Hurst equalised for England. Towards the end of the second half, Martin Peters' goal put England 2–1 in the lead. The boys were ecstatic! Then disaster struck, West Germany scored from a free kick just before full time. Tony was next to some German fans.

⬇ England captain, Bobby Moore, holds the World Cup trophy as the team celebrate.

> *When they equalised two enormous German fans embraced each other and I was in the middle. I was going, 'guuurrrrhhhh'. I was being crushed and Mike grabbed me out from the middle.*

Then it was the English fans' turn to celebrate. Geoff Hurst scored in extra time, then scored again seconds before the final whistle, giving England a famous 4–2 victory.

VICTORY

Tony remembers how the victory felt.

> *We went mental at the final whistle. We were chanting, 'Ee, ay, adiyo, we won the cup' for hours and hours. I couldn't convey to anyone how wonderful it was to have been there – the emotion of it all. It was the most wonderful moment in the history of the universe!*

SUPERPOWERS

During the 1960s, America and Russia were rival superpowers. The rest of the world looked on as they built up stocks of nuclear weapons and competed to be the first to send a man to the moon.

THE CUBAN MISSILE CRISIS

In 1960, John F Kennedy became the youngest ever American president. He took on heavy responsibilities. In October 1962, he was faced with an international crisis. American spy planes discovered that Russia was sending missiles to the island of Cuba in the Caribbean. Kennedy threatened to invade Cuba unless Russia withdrew the missiles.

Man on the moon
• •

On 12th April 1961, a Russian, Yuri Gagarin, became the first man in space. President Kennedy responded by promising that America would land a man on the moon before the end of the decade.

On 20th July 1969, hundreds of millions of people all over the world watched on television as American astronaut Neil Armstrong stepped out of the lunar module onto the moon with the famous words, 'That's one small step for man, one giant leap for mankind'. Alasdair was on holiday in France with friends from university.

Tony remembers being terrified.

> " *We heard it on the television and radio and read about it in the newspapers. My parents talked about it all the time. We really thought a nuclear war was going to start. I remember coming home from school and deciding the best place to go was behind the fridge, and pulling the fridge out and hiding behind it.* "

After an anxious week of talks, the Russians backed down and withdrew their missiles.

"*We sat there with Scandinavians, Germans and lots of French people. We watched on TV as history unfolded in front of our eyes. Everyone felt it was something mankind had achieved, it wasn't just an American show. We just felt part of a huge global family.*"

ASSASSINATION

On 22nd November 1963, John F Kennedy was shot and killed as he drove through Dallas, Texas in an open car. The suspected assassin was shot and killed two days later while he was in police custody. Questions about the death of the president still remain unanswered.

The event was so shocking that people all over the world can still remember where they were when they heard the terrible news.

⬆ Kennedy, seated on the back seat with his wife, Jacqueline, moments before he was assassinated.

MIKE

" *On the day Kennedy was killed, I was at boarding school near a military air base. At first, everyone assumed the Russians had shot him. All through that night we heard military planes going over and we were saying, 'Do we hide under the bed or what?' It was a very frightening night.* "

ALASDAIR

" *Kennedy was alive when I left for a boy-scout meeting. By the time I got there, 20 minutes later, the news had broken. Everybody was standing around not knowing what to do. Nobody had any heart for doing anything because one of the most charismatic leaders in the world had died.* "

TONY

" *I went to see the* Harry Worth Show *[a TV comedy] being recorded in Manchester. At the end of the recording, someone came on and said, 'We've got some bad news to tell you. President Kennedy's been assassinated.' We'd been promised fish and chips on the way home but we didn't stop, we were so shocked.* "

Wales in the 1960s

PENARTH

Diana was 12 in 1960 and her sister Sue was 14. They grew up in Penarth, a coal port on the Severn Estuary in south Wales. By the 1960s, Penarth was no longer a working coal port. Even though only a few small, coastal coal boats used the harbour, Diana remembers that the water was very polluted.

> *There was a pebble beach and promenade with a pier. In those days the water was brown because of suspended mud and coal dust but it didn't deter us from jumping from the pier at high tide, swimming in it and dinghy sailing on it.*

FROTHY COFFEE

There were plenty of meeting places along the waterside promenade for Diana and her friends to get together and drink frothy coffee.

> *Along the 'prom' there was an Italian Garden with palm trees, cafés, a coffee bar with a juke box, an Italian ice-cream parlour and restaurants. Frothy coffee was popular – what's new with cappuccino?*

Diana Caryl's story

Diana, 1968

NATIONAL EISTEDDFOD

Diana went several times on school trips to the National Eisteddfod – the Welsh international music competition – at Llangollen.

> *I was fascinated by the choirs from far-away places in exotic costumes, and seeing Welsh people in national costume as well. It wouldn't have the same impact now as children see so much on TV, but to see South American Indians in the flesh, performing their strange music with strange instruments, was wonderful and opened our eyes to the world beyond our life.*

WELSH MINING

During the 1960s, coal mining in south Wales was still a major industry. Now there is only one working coal mine in the area. Diana remembers driving through the Welsh valleys and past mining villages on the way to the Eisteddfod.

> 66 *All the villages looked the same: giant pithead wheels and rows of terraced houses with shining doorsteps and brass knockers. But there was a general air of grime from the coal dust. There were black slag heaps on the surrounding hillsides with bracken and heather-covered slopes beyond.* 99

⬇ Rescue workers digging among the rubble and mud covering the Aberfan school.

ABERFAN DISASTER

Slag – waste from the mines – was piled up at the pitheads in heaps the size of small hills. On 21st October 1966, a slag heap on the edge of the mining village of Aberfan slipped and buried the village primary school under tons of debris and coal dust. 116 children and 28 adults were killed.

> 66 *Several of my teachers went to help the Women's Voluntary Service and told us how harrowing it was. We felt it particularly as it involved children. We saw on TV the devastation of an area that looked perfectly normal and natural to us.* 99

After the tragedy, steps were taken to make the slag heaps safer.

Work and houses

JOB FOR LIFE

Before the 1960s a job had always been regarded as a job for life. Young people chose a profession or a trade when they left school and were expected to stick at it until they retired. Many school leavers became apprentices, which meant they were taken on by a company and trained while they worked and were being paid. Others went into the family business. During the 1960s, all this began to change.

When Valerie changed her job, her father didn't approve.

↑ A steel works at Ebbw Vale in Wales, 1966.

> " *I remember Daddy being very shocked when I said I was going to move my job because at that time, you joined a job and you stayed in it for life.* "

STEEL WORKERS

Diana remembers the steel industry in Wales was still providing work. But these jobs were not going to be for life. Steel works, like the mines, began to close down. It was hard for the coal and steel workers to get other jobs in the area where they had been brought up.

> " *The steel industry was still strong in Newport and Swansea. In the mid-1960s a neighbour's son went off to become an apprentice roll-turner in the steelworks and it was considered a good trade – no hint of what was to come.* "

Alasdair remembers there were plenty of what were called 'blue-collar jobs' – factory and manual work – in the area around Dumfries.

> " *There was a huge ICI chemicals factory, a rubber works which made rubber tyres and the Carnation milk factory where the product of all the cows from many miles around was converted into very sticky, sweet Carnation milk.* "

But for those with university degrees there was less choice in the area. Only two of Alasdair's friends found work in Dumfries.

> " *We had to leave Dumfries because it was too small for us to get work. We had to go to the big cities in Scotland and England.* "

HOUSING

Towns and cities were expanding. They spread out, taking over the surrounding countryside as new housing was built on the outskirts. John remembers how his life was disrupted when the family business relocated to what was called the executive belt and the family moved house.

> " *Land in the Manchester City green belt was released for building and you could buy land and build on it. My parents bought land and built a bungalow.* "

John has never moved far but his children have had a very different experience.

> " *The world has shrunk to the size of a pea now. I live and work near to where I was born. Now families fully expect their children to move away to find jobs.* "

! Diana remembers...
"Estates were built on greenfield sites around Penarth and big houses were turned into flats. Many residents were commuters to nearby Cardiff, including my father who was an optician."

← High-rise flats under construction in Glasgow, 1960.

Timeline

1960
21st March South African police kill 69 and wound 180 Africans demonstrating against Pass Laws in what became known as the Sharpeville Massacre.
9th November John F Kennedy is elected president of America.

1961
12th April Russian Yuri Gagarin becomes the first man in space.
August Western powers protest as the Berlin Wall goes up, dividing communist East and democratic West Berlin.
17th September 850 people arrested in London's biggest ever ban-the-bomb demonstration.

1962
5th August Film star Marilyn Monroe is found dead at her home in Hollywood.
5th October The Beatles release their first hit single 'Love Me Do'.
October The Cuban missile crisis. It ends on 28 October when Russia withdraws.

1963
28th October Martin Luther King delivers his 'I have a dream' speech to 200,000 peaceful demonstrators in Washington.
22nd November President Kennedy is assassinated in Dallas, Texas.
24th November Lee Harvey Oswald, suspected of assassinating Kennedy, is shot dead by Jack Ruby, an escaped convict, while in the hands of the police.

1964
8th February The Beatles are mobbed by fans at Kennedy Airport in New York.
14th June In South Africa, Nelson Mandela is imprisoned on Robben Island.
16th October In Britain, Harold Wilson leads the Labour Party to election victory.

1965
30th January Sir Winston Churchill's funeral is held in St Paul's Cathedral, London.
26th October The Beatles receive MBEs.

1966
30th July England football team win the World Cup at Wembley.
27th October 116 children and 28 adults die when a slag heap buries a school in Aberfan.

1967
10th June Israel wins the Six Day War against neighbouring Arab states.
3rd December The first ever successful heart transplant is carried out in South Africa.

1968
17th March Anti-war demonstrators storm the American Embassy in London.
4th April Martin Luther King is assassinated in Memphis, Tennessee.
22nd August Russia crushes a rebellion against their occupation of Czechoslovakia.

1969
9th April Supersonic airliner Concorde makes its maiden test flight.
21st July The first manned moon-landing.

Glossary

Applied maths The study of mathematics and its practical application to the natural world and things around us.

Assassinated To be murdered, usually for political or religious reasons.

Authority The power to tell other people what they should do and how they should behave.

Boutique A small shop selling fashionable clothes.

Charismatic Having personal qualities that allows a person to attract and influence others.

Civil rights The rights of all citizens to have personal freedom and equal political, social and legal rights.

Coal port A town by the sea or a river which takes in coal or sends it abroad in ships.

Communist Someone who believes in Communism – a system where no one owns private property.

Cult A religious belief or an idea that attracts a group of devoted followers.

Executive belt A band of houses on the outskirts of a town for people with management jobs in businesses.

Generation People within a certain age group. Teenagers are from a younger generation than their parents and teachers.

Global family The idea that everyone in the world belongs to one enormous family.

Hadrian's Wall A wall built by the Roman Emperor Hadrian nearly 2,000 years ago on the border between Scotland and England.

Household appliances Machines such as washing machines and refrigerators.

Inhibitions Feelings that stop you from acting freely or saying what you think.

Missiles Weapons that are fired from a powerful gun or launched by a rocket.

Nuclear weapons Weapons that have very high explosive power.

Phenomenon A remarkable or unusual event. Beatlemania was a phenomenon because it was an extraordinary event that had never happened before.

Pithead wheel A huge wheel at the entrance to a coal mine that turns to lower and raise mining equipment in and out of the pit.

Profession A job for which you need training, such as a teacher, doctor or lawyer.

Promenade A paved area in a seaside town where people can walk along the seafront.

Scottish Highlanders People who live in the Scottish Highlands (a mountainous region in north-west Scotland).

Scullery A small room attached to a kitchen for doing jobs such as the washing-up or peeling vegetables.

Superpowers Very powerful countries with nuclear weapons.

Index